NORTH AMERICA

Troll Associates

NORTH AMERICA

by Louis Sabin
Illustrated by Allan Eitzen

Troll Associates

Library of Congress Cataloging in Publication Data

Sabin, Louis.
  North America.

  Summary: Describes the physical characteristics,
climate, natural resources, and cultures of the North
American continent.
    1. North America—Description and travel—Juvenile
literature. [1. North America] I. Eitzen, Allan, ill.
II. Title.
E41.S23   1985   917   84-8625
ISBN 0-8167-0240-3 (lib. bdg.)
ISBN 0-8167-0241-1 (pbk.)

North America is not the largest continent on Earth, but in many ways it is the most beautiful. From the glittering ice-world of northern Canada and Greenland to the lush green jungles of Central America, the continent is blessed with natural beauty.

7

There are rolling hills and lofty mountains, vast prairies, broad rivers, and shimmering lakes. And there are sun-baked deserts, yawning canyons, thick forests, and a treasure of minerals and wildlife.

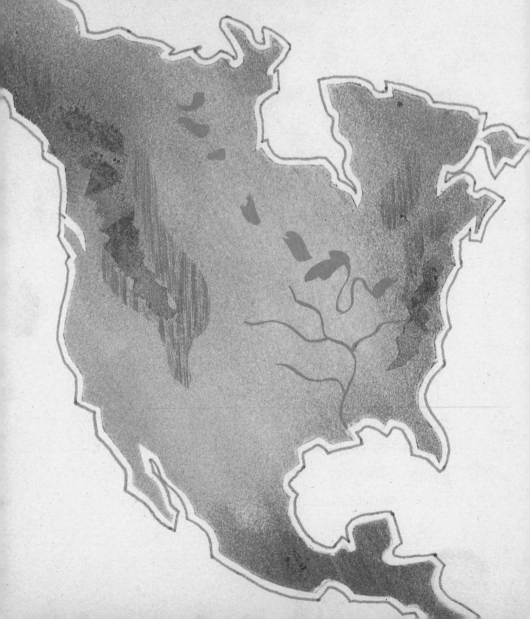

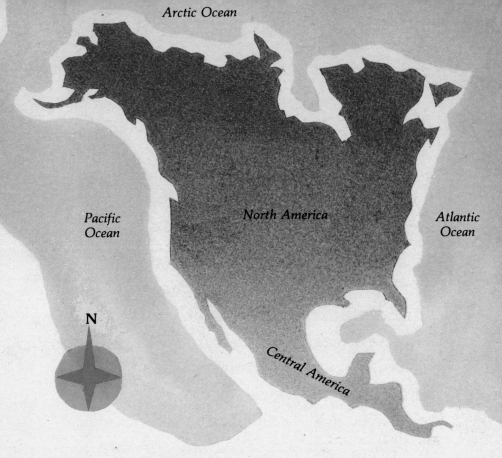

The third largest continent, after Asia and Africa, North America is shaped something like a triangle. Its widest part faces north and is bounded by the Arctic Ocean. The two long sides of the triangle are bordered by the Pacific Ocean to the west and the Atlantic Ocean to the east. The triangle points south, and at its point is the narrow strip of land called Central America. Central America connects the continent to South America.

Aleutians

There are also a number of islands that are counted as part of North America. To the north are dozens of islands in the Arctic. To the northeast, the largest islands are Greenland and Newfoundland. To the east and south are Bermuda and the West Indies, which include Cuba, Hispaniola, Jamaica, and the Bahamas. And along the west and northwest are Vancouver Island and a series of smaller islands that end with the Aleutians off Alaska.

North America has a wide range of climates, soils, minerals, vegetation, animal life, and land forms. The northernmost regions are polar or subpolar. For example, in Greenland, the Canadian islands far to the north, and in much of Alaska, winter temperatures are usually far below zero.

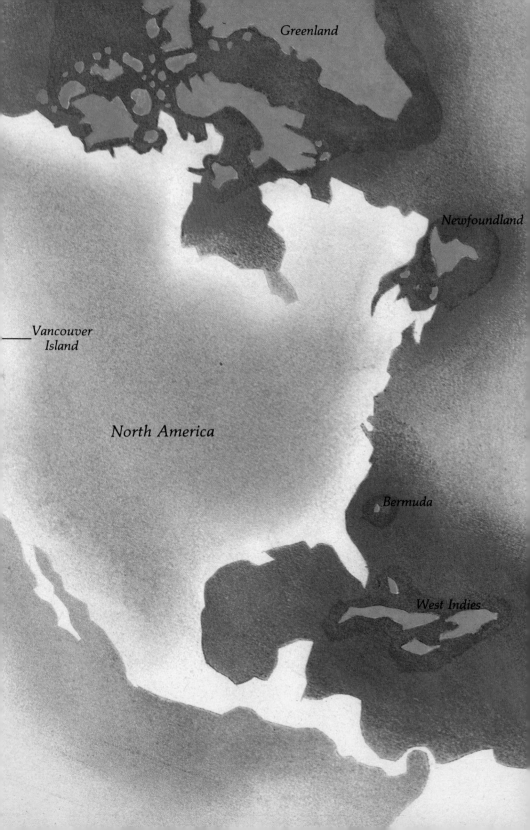

Some areas of the far north are snow-covered all year long, while the treeless tundras have a brief, cool summer. At times during the summer, warm winds from the Pacific Ocean bring some relief to parts of Alaska. Then grasses grow and flowers bloom.

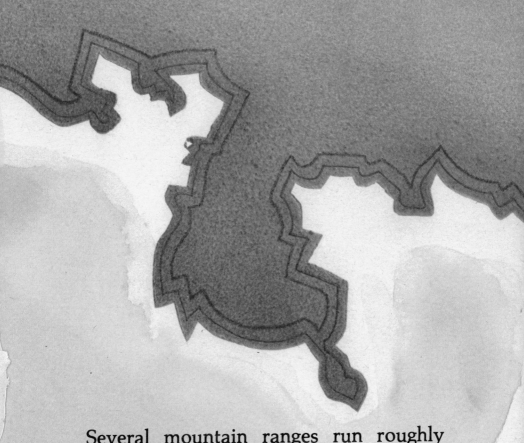

Several mountain ranges run roughly parallel to the western coastline of North America. They include the Cascades, the Sierra Nevada, the Coast Mountains, the Alaska Range, and the Olympic Mountains. Here are ice-tipped peaks as well as the active volcano, Mount Saint Helens. Southeast lies the Great Basin, which includes Death Valley, the lowest point in North America.

Pacific Ocean

East of the Great Basin, the Rocky Mountains run down the continent like a gigantic backbone. The Rockies form the Continental Divide. Any rain that falls on the western slopes of the Rockies runs westward—toward the Pacific Ocean. Precipitation that falls on the eastern slopes of the Rockies, however, finds its way toward the other side of the continent—into the Atlantic Ocean, the Arctic Ocean, or the Gulf of Mexico.

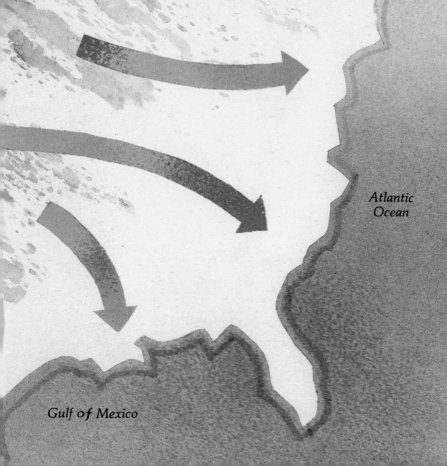

Atlantic Ocean

Gulf of Mexico

The Missouri and Mississippi Rivers form the longest river system in North America, draining much of the area between the Rockies and the Appalachian Mountains near the east coast. This huge area is a vast interior plain known as the Great Plains, or the Midwest.

Here, the winters are cold and snowy, and the summers range from warm to hot. This area leads the world in producing grain and in raising livestock. Grain and meat from this great lowland region are shipped everywhere, while also supplying North Americans with the most abundant diet on Earth.

The climate in the region from the Appalachian Mountains to the east coast of North America has blustery, cold winters and warm summers. Farming accounts for some of the productivity in this stretch of land. So does Atlantic Ocean fishing.

Appalachian Mountains

Atlantic Ocean

But the greatest wealth of the Northeast lies in its excellent natural harbors along the coast and the rivers that run to the ocean. Important commercial and industrial cities have grown up throughout this part of the continent.

Farther south, the temperatures in both winter and summer are warmer than those in the north. This region is often called the Sun Belt. In recent years the population of the Sun Belt has been rising rapidly. Cities such as Dallas, Atlanta, Phoenix, and San Diego have grown larger every year. One reason is their pleasant southern and southwestern climate.

Much of Mexico, which lies still farther south, also has a climate that is pleasant throughout the year. Along the coasts of the Pacific Ocean and the Gulf of Mexico, the weather is warm. In the mountains and plateaus in the center of the country, it is usually cool and dry. Only at the narrow, southern end of Mexico and in Central America is it always very warm and moist. The vegetation in this area and in the Caribbean Islands is tropical, with jungles and rain forests that stay green and lush all year.

The natural resources of North America are enormous. Its mines produce more copper, iron, silver, lead, coal, and salt than any other place on Earth. In addition, there are large supplies of gold, zinc, nickel, natural gas, and oil.

North America has the raw materials needed to make cars and household appliances and other manufactured products. It also has the fuel to power the factories that make those products. And these two things —raw materials and fuel—have made North America an industrial giant.

Along with its natural resources and excellent farm land, North America has a network of waterways that make transportation and shipping easy, even over large stretches of land.

The Great Lakes, on the United States-Canadian border, form the largest body of fresh water in the world. And with their connecting arms through the St. Lawrence River, the Mississippi-Missouri river system, and the Illinois waterway, they form a web of water routes that runs thousands of miles.

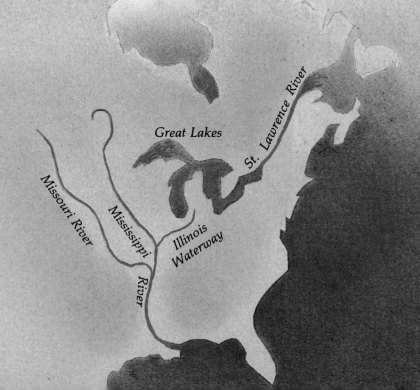

A ship can carry Canadian wheat all the way from Thunder Bay, Ontario, down to New Orleans and out to the Gulf of Mexico. Or it can carry cars from Detroit out to the Gulf of St. Lawrence, then into the North Atlantic Ocean.

North America is also crisscrossed by a web of modern roads and highways, railroad lines, and air routes.

North America has always been a leader in science and technology. Atomic energy, computer science, space exploration, telecommunications, and many advances in medical treatment are among the technological and scientific contributions made by North Americans.

There are still very poor and uneducated people in parts of North America—people who lack jobs and medical care, whose living conditions and health standards need to be improved. But efforts are being made to help these people.

There are free public schools in much of North America, as well as fine universities, colleges, and technical schools. Modern medical care is also available in most regions of the continent. These factors, combined with widespread economic opportunities, continue to improve the standard of life in North America.

North America has also contributed greatly to the arts. Movies, television, radio, and other forms of entertainment and information originated in North America. The continent has also given the world the airplane, the steamboat, the telephone, the electric light, the phonograph, and many other inventions.

North America is called a young continent because its modern character has been developing for less than five hundred years. But it has made giant steps in that time. And with its vast wealth of people, land, and natural resources, its future promises to be as bright as its past.